STORY TALK 2

Sheila Freeman and Esther Munns

MACMILLAN

CONTENTS

PICKING UP CLUES

Games with books	4
Play games with words	8
Which came first – joke or poem?	10
A story starts here	12
Dipping into a ghost story	16
Jacob Two-Two meets The Hooded Fang	20

IF AT FIRST YOU DO NOT SEE

A picture riddle – boy or bird?	26
What's in a name?	28
What's in a shape?	29
What's in a poem?	30
Hodgeheg	32
Going spaces is good for you	36
Going places is good for you	42

STORY TALK

There's nothing to do – I'm bored	46
A story ... man!	50
Talk in stories	54
Stories in quilts and bedspreads and even wallpaper	58

DROP EVERYTHING AND READ

Ramona Quimby, aged eight	66
Amanda	70
Long legs or long ears?	72
A poster poem	73
A hamster at large	74

PICKING UP CLUES

GAMES WITH BOOKS

Starting to play a new board game is a bit like starting to read a new book. On page 6 you will find out why.

the Jacob Two Two game for Two or Two+Two Players

The Greengrocer is insulted. Run away to Richmond Park. ↑2 **10**	**11**		**3**
9	**12**		**2**
8	Fall asleep in Richmond Park. MISS 2 TURNS **13**		
Sent on first errand for 2 Pounds of Tomatoes. ↑2 **7**	**14**		
6	**15**	Meal of stale bread and shaving water.	**2**
5	Taken to court Louis the loser defends you. ↑2 **16**		**2**
Fall off two wheel bike. Big People laugh. 2↓4	Master Fish and Mistress Fowl row you to Slimers Isle. 2↓17		**2**
3	Given Supersonic Bleeper by Child power score × TWO. **18**	Meet the Hooded Fang. Laugh at him.	
2	**19**		**2**
Jacob Two Two a little person. **1**	Arrive at Slimers Isle. THIS WAY SLIMERS ISLE From which NO BRATS RETURN MISS 2 TURNS **20**		

4

PICKING UP CLUES

se bleeper. most give up hope of rescue. **MISS 2 TURNS** 31	FOG a tiny cloud. 50	51
32	49	Hug Hooded Fang. ↓2 52
33	48	53
ken to g Factory ↑2 34	47	Sun comes out. 54
35	Fog disappears. ↑2 46	55
36	45	56
tenced to be wn to crocodiles. ↑2 37	44	57
38	Child Power to the rescue! Crocodiles dead ↑2 43	wake up in Richmond Park **MISS 2 TURNS** 58
39	42	59
meal - chops and tub deserts **MISS 2 TURNS** 40	41	2 Pounds of Tomatoes. 60

RULES

Play with a dice

To start, Throw 2 × 2 + 2 (6)

🌫 FOG
means - go back 2

☀
means - go Forward 2

Before you start playing a new board game, it is a good idea to read the rules and to look carefully at the board and at any pictures on the board. All these things will give you clues to help you get started.

On pages 4 and 5 you saw a board game we made up from a story called *Jacob Two-Two meets The Hooded Fang*.

In pairs look carefully at the board. Read the rules. Decide what you need to play the game. Together, try to work out anything you don't understand.

Look at the front and back covers of the book. You will find more clues there to help you.

When you are
ready, begin
playing the game.

Discuss what you have learnt about the story from playing the game and from looking at the front and back covers of the book.

Take it in turns to see how much of the story you can tell each other.

You could make up parts of the story. Try to describe Jacob's meeting with the Greengrocer, Master Fish and Mistress Fowl, and The Hooded Fang. Guess what each character looks like, what each one says to Jacob and how Jacob feels at different times in his adventure.

If you would like to find out what happens to Jacob Two-Two in prison, you can read about it on pages 20–23.

PICKING UP CLUES

General Editor: Aidan Chambers

Jacob Two-Two Meets the Hooded Fang

Jacob Two-Two stared up into the awful face of the prison warden — the dreaded Hooded Fang.

'Remove the prisoner to the lowest, dampest dungeon,' growled the Hooded Fang. 'And put him on a diet of stale bread and water.'

Jacob's future looks bleak. But though he is small and young and tends to say things twice, he is far from being a coward. And when the Infamous Two come to his aid, even the Hooded Fang has to look out.

How Jacob gets himself into prison and why, and how he gets himself out again with the help of CHILD POWER is all part of this funny and eventful story.

M books

Macmillan Education

ISBN 0-333-42916-8

PLAY GAMES WITH WORDS

Who tells the best jokes in your class?

On these pages there are some jokes, limericks, puns, tongue-twisters and riddles. Can you say which is which?

Hold a contest to find the best tongue-twister in the class.

Mother: Please keep quiet, Tom. Your father's trying to read.
Tom: Crikey, I learnt how to do that years ago.

Q: Did you think everything went into the Ark in pairs?
A: Well, the worms went in apples.

Swan swam over the sea,
Swim, swan, swim,
Swan swum back again,
Well swum, swan.

Q: Why were the bees on strike?
A: Shorter flowers and more honey.

Collect your favourite jokes, tongue-twisters and riddles.

Drop them into a GAMES WITH WORDS BOX for others to share.

"Open wide," said a
dentist called Bert.
To a man-eating shark
whose teeth hurt.
"When I've finished drilling
I'll give you a filling".
He did — and the
...

Q: What do baby apes sleep in?
A: Apricots.

The Terns
Said the mother Tern
to her baby Tern,
"Would you like a baby brother?"
Said the baby Tern
to mother Tern,
"Yes, one good Tern
deserves
another."

PICKING UP CLUES

Little Nancy Netticoat
Wears a white petticoat.
The longer she lives,
The shorter she grows,
Little Nancy Netticoat.

Write out another riddle for the:

GAMES WITH WORDS BOX

Here are words to help you make a "punny" joke!

cheep   cheap
tail   tale
knight   night

This is a "droodle": What is it?

And this is another: What is it?

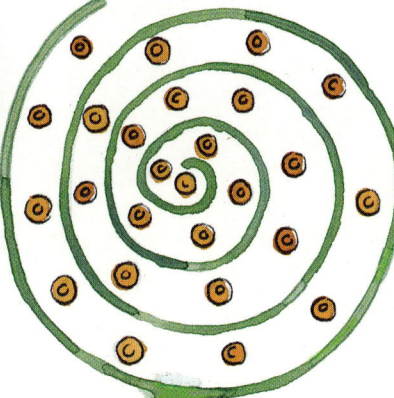

Can you make up and draw another "droodle"? Drop it in a:

DROODLE BOX

A giraffe going past a window.

Lots of Mexicans going up a hill.

WHICH CAME FIRST– JOKE OR POEM?

On these pages there's a poem that gives you clues on how to make up a joke, and a joke that gives you clues on how to finish a poem.

With a friend, share the joke and finish the poem.

First, practise reading aloud this poem by Spike Milligan. One of you can be the baby sardine, the other the mum.

A baby sardine
Saw her first submarine;
She was scared and watched through a peephole.

"Oh, come, come, come,"
Said the sardine's mum,
"It's only a tin full of people."

Now use the illustration and the clues from the poem to help you complete this joke:

What did the ____ say when she saw a ____?
"Look, mum _____."

Read the next joke with your friend. Then use it to help you fill in the missing words from the poem underneath, by Gregory Harrison. Do not use the same word twice.

PICKING UP CLUES

Mum: Come on, John, eat your breakfast; you'll be late for school.
John: I don't want to go to school. The teachers don't like me, the children don't like me – even the caretaker doesn't like me!
Mum: All the same, you must go.
John: Why should I?
Mum: Well, for one thing you're forty-five years old, and for another you're the headmaster!

Distracted, the ____ said to her boy,
"Do you try to upset and perplex and annoy?
Now, give me four reasons – and don't play the fool –
Why you shouldn't get up and get ready for ____."

Her ____ replied slowly, "Well, mother, you see,
I can't stand the ____ and they ____ me;
And there isn't a ____ or a girl in the ____
That I ____ or, in turn, that delights in my face."

"And I'll give you two ____," she said, "why you ought
Get yourself off to school before you get caught;
Because, first, you are forty, and, ____, you young fool,
It's your ____ to be there.
You're the ____ of the school."

11

A STORY STARTS HERE

How do you choose a book to read?

When we asked children of your age this question, these are some of the things they said:

I go by the cover – if it looks exciting I read the bit inside.

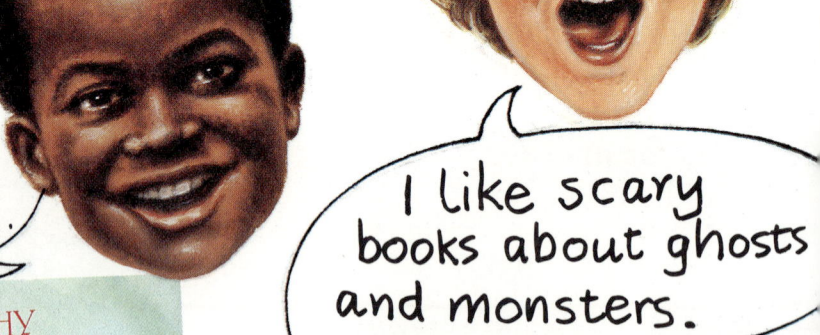

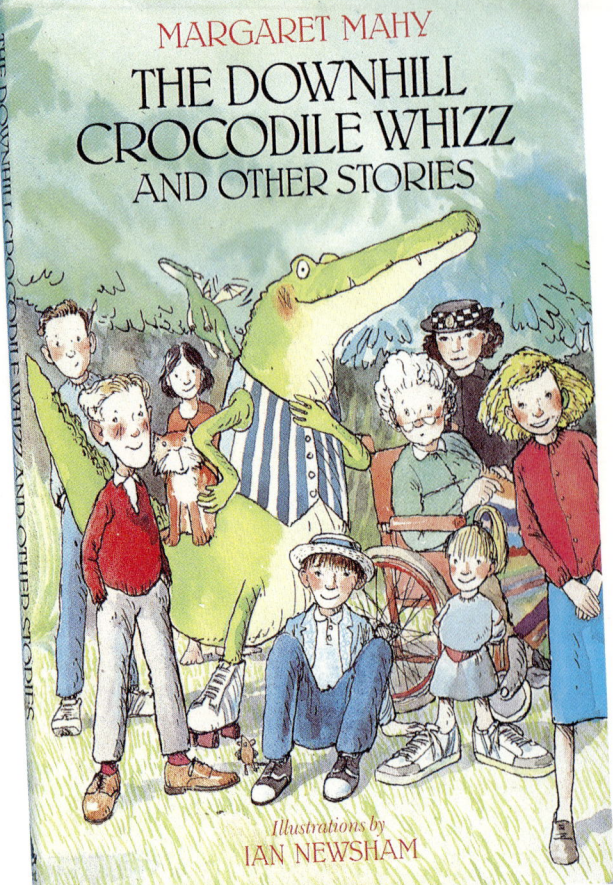

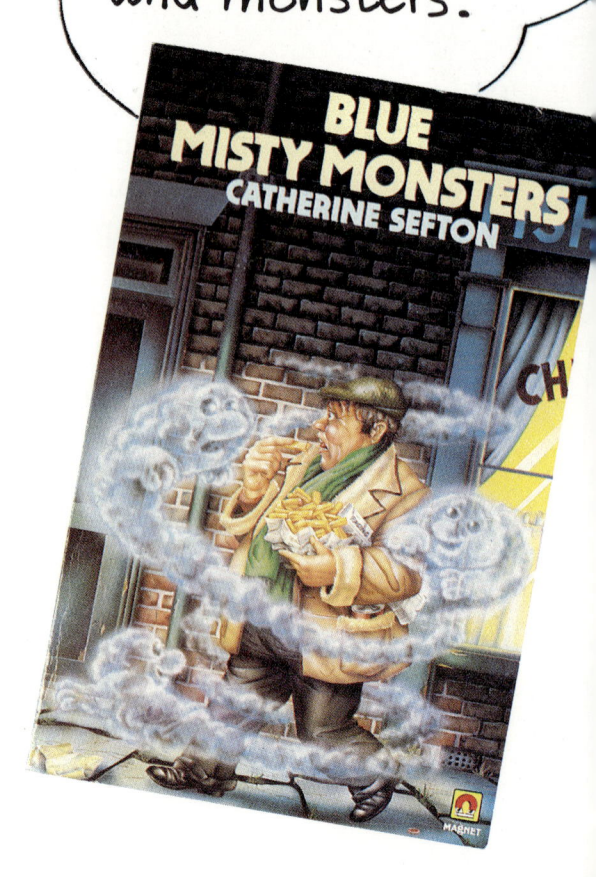

I like scary books about ghosts and monsters.

I always read the title first and imagine what the story is about.

My favourite author is ick King-Smith, so I look for one of his that I haven't read.

Everyone we asked thought the cover was very important — "like an advertisement".

Here are some covers and other clues to introduce four books to you. Talk about each book. Which one would you most like to read?

What helped you to make up your mind?

PICKING UP CLUES

Snakes and Ladders
poems about the ups and downs of life by
ROBIN KLEIN

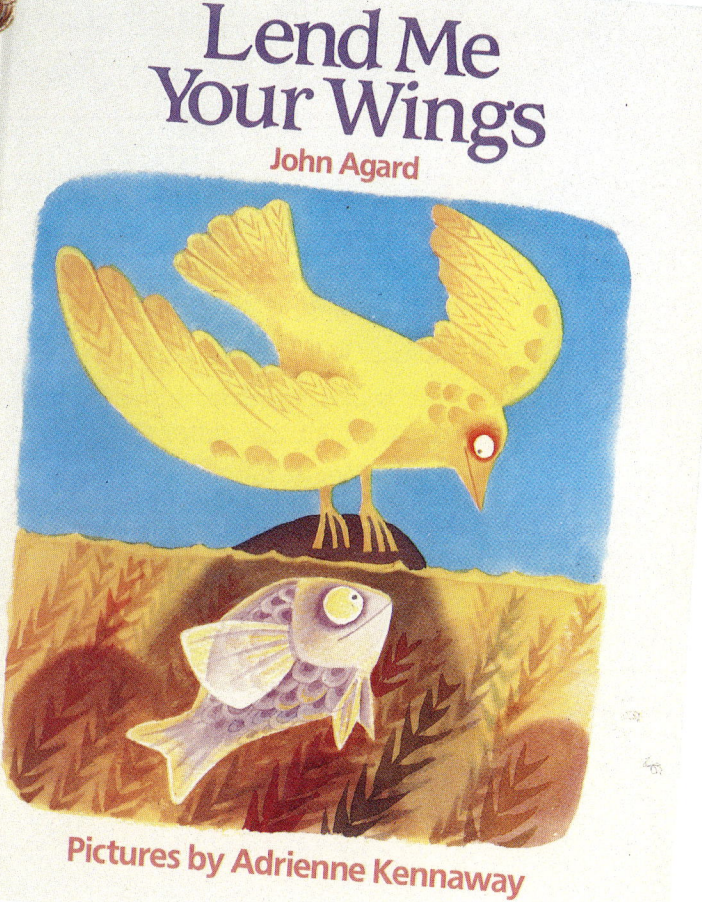

Lend Me Your Wings
John Agard
Pictures by Adrienne Kennaway

PHILIPPA PEARCE
The Elm Street Lot

The gang of children who meet on Elm Street are always in on the action, whether it's tracking down a lost hamster or going on safari across the roof-tops.

By the author of *Minnow on the Say* and *Tom's Midnight Garden*.

Illustrated by Peter Rush

U.K. £1.10
AUST. $2.95 (recommended)
N.Z. $4.50
CAN. $3.95

ISBN 0 14 03.1147 5

A Puffin Book
Published by Penguin Books

BACK   FRONT

Look carefully at the book covers on these two pages. They belong to two different copies of the same story.

Make a list of all the differences between the illustrations of the two copies and the writing that goes with them.
   Sometimes when a book is reprinted, the cover is changed. Which of these covers is the new one? Why do you think the publishers changed the cover?

Choose a book you have enjoyed and would like to persuade your friends to read. Show them the cover. Ask them to guess what the story might be about. Introduce the story to them by reading aloud the beginning. Stop at a place which will make your listeners want to go on reading for themselves.

14

A YOUNG PUFFIN

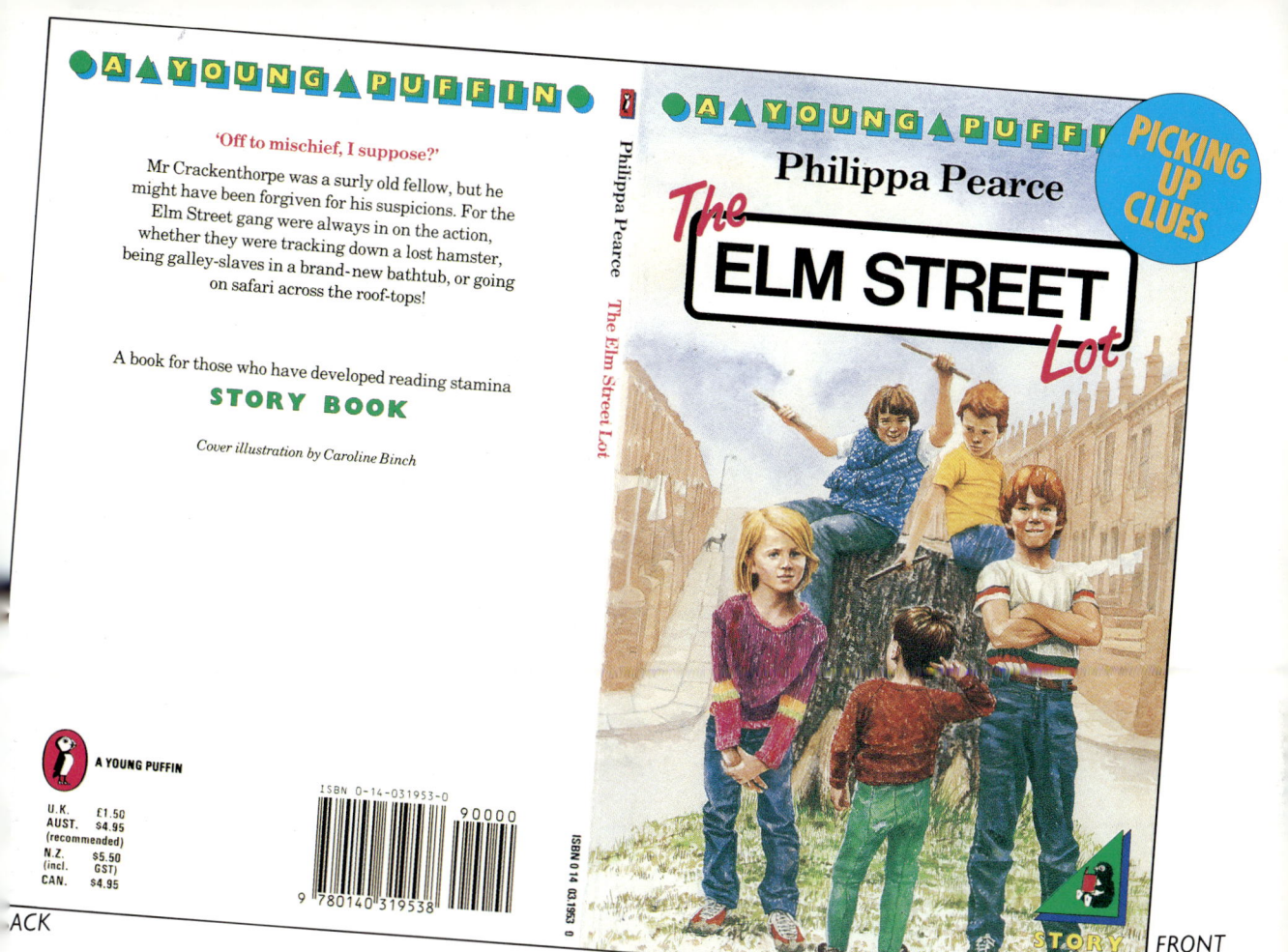

A YOUNG PUFFIN

PICKING UP CLUES

'Off to mischief, I suppose?'

Mr Crackenthorpe was a surly old fellow, but he might have been forgiven for his suspicions. For the Elm Street gang were always in on the action, whether they were tracking down a lost hamster, being galley-slaves in a brand-new bathtub, or going on safari across the roof-tops!

A book for those who have developed reading stamina

STORY BOOK

Cover illustration by Caroline Binch

Philippa Pearce

The ELM STREET Lot

A YOUNG PUFFIN

U.K. £1.50
AUST. $4.95 (recommended)
N.Z. $5.50 (incl. GST)
CAN. $4.95

ISBN 0-14-031953-0

9 780140 319538

BACK   FRONT

Read again a story you have enjoyed.

Design a new book cover for it.

Write a few sentences of your own to go on the back of your cover. Give some clues about the kind of story it is, but don't spoil your readers' enjoyment by telling them too much!

DIPPING INTO A GHOST STORY

Have you ever found that dipping into a story sometimes makes you want to read all of it?

Read this exciting part from the middle of the book *Storm*.

When they came to the ford, Annie asked Willa about the ghost.

"He's here, all right. He's here," said Willa. "You know the story."

"What story?" asked Annie.

"When he was alive – I mean when he had a body – he used to own Mr Elkins' farm. That was in the days when there were highwaymen. Two of them ambushed him right here."

Annie felt a cold finger slowly moving from the base of her spine up to her neck, and then spreading out across her shoulders.

"Where we're standing," said Willa.

"What happened?" asked Annie.

"He wouldn't give them his money," said Willa. "He was that brave. So they killed him and his horse."

"His horse!" cried Annie. "That's horrible!" And at once she began to think of her lonely walks back from school – the dark January journeys lying in wait for her.

"So they got his money anyhow," said Willa. "That's what I've heard."

"And the ghost?" said Annie.

"That goes up and down and around and pays out passers by," said Willa. The sisters fell silent and stared at the flashing water.

On the third night after Willa came home there was a tremendous storm. Annie lay warm in her bed and listened to the wind going wild outside. It bumped and blundered against the walls of the cottage, it whistled between its salty lips and gnashed its sharp teeth.

As Annie dozed, she began to imagine she was not in bed but in a boat, rocking, quite safe, far out at sea. The sheets of rain lashing at her little window were small waves smacking at the bows, streaming down the boat's sides . . .

This was the night on which Willa's baby decided to be born.

Tell each other all that you have found out about Annie and where she lives. In small groups, make guesses about how the story might continue. See how many different ideas you can think of. Jot down all your ideas on a big piece of paper for everyone to see.

Here are some clues to help you:

1 Look at the front cover of the book.

2 Read the "About this book" section.

About this book
On a wild, stormy night, Annie is offered a ride by a tall, silent horseman. She overcomes her fear of the ghost who is said to haunt the lonely road and accepts the ride – but who is this mysterious stranger?

About the author
Kevin Crossley-Holland's books for children include *The Dead Moon*, a collection of folk tales, and *Beowulf*. He also writes for adults and is a poet and a regular broadcaster for the BBC.

He lives with his wife and two-year-old daughter, Œnone, in an old house in Suffolk, and has two grown-up sons.

STORM
Kevin Crossley-Holland

A BANANA BOOK

ILLUSTRATED BY
ALAN MARKS

PICKING UP CLUES

3 "'Willa says Rod can't get home now until early in the New Year,' said Annie's mother."

4 "'I wouldn't like to marry a sailor,' said Annie."

5 "Annie's parents were rather old and not too well."

6 "Mr Carter banged the telephone with the palm of his hand. He listened again. There was not a sound."

Choose one of your group's ideas which fits all the clues, then decide how to end your story.
   Share your story with other groups in the class.

JACOB TWO-TWO MEETS THE HOODED FANG

You have already met these two characters in the board game on pages 4–5 and on the book cover on page 6. You will remember how Jacob Two-Two found himself face to face with the horrible Hooded Fang.

Jacob was sentenced to spend two years, two months, two weeks, two days, two minutes in the darkest dungeons of the children's prison. Every day he was forced to make goods in the prison workshops. All eleven goods on the list were designed to make life miserable for children. Here are five; can you think of six others?

1 Jigsaw puzzles too complicated to solve
2 No-flow ketchup, guaranteed to stick in the bottle
3 Dentists' drills
4 Bad-temper pills for teachers and babysitters
5 Rain for picnics

Read Chapter 11, the part of the story where clever Jacob manages to make The Hooded Fang into a two-two person. Can you work out what a two-two person is?

Jacob Two-Two was not only overworked and hungry most of the time, but he was also in ever-deepening trouble with The Hooded Fang. The Fang, it appeared had come to detest him more than all the other prisoners.

"That lousy Jacob Two-Two," complained The Hooded Fang bitterly to his wife one night, "will be the end of me. When I pass, he doesn't cower, shiver, or even tremble, but instead puts a hand to his mouth to suppress a giggle."

PICKING UP CLUES

Mrs Hooded Fang was outraged. "But hasn't he seen all the signs on the prison grounds, saying you're vile, inhuman, and vicious?"

"The little stinker," cried The Hooded Fang, "was brought up not to believe everything he reads. Furthermore, I can't even get him to admit his age. Whenever I ask him how old he is, he says," and here The Hooded Fang mimicked Jacob Two-Two, "'Why, I'm two plus two plus two years old'. Worse news. He won't answer his cell door *unless I knock two times*."

"Punish him!"

"But no punishment works."

"Have you tried making him eat soup with a fork?"

"I've tried everything. I must break his spirit, you see, and the only way I can do that is to get him to say anything but two. If only I could get him to say one, three, or even sixteen. Sixteen!" exclaimed The Hooded Fang. "That's it!" And he leaped up, knocking over his wife, and charging out of his lair and down the two hundred steps to Jacob Two-Two's cell, remembering to knock two times.

"All right, Jacob Two-Two," said The Hooded Fang, "if you're such a clever little fellow, can you tell me how many legs I've got?"

"Why, two, of course," said Jacob Two-Two. "Why, two, of course."

"Good. First-rate. And now, Jacob Two-Two," said The Hooded Fang, hard put to conceal a fiendish grin, "can you tell me how many suns there are?"

"Aside from me," said Jacob Two-Two twice, "my father has two. Daniel and Noah."

"No, you twerp! Suns. *S-u-n*. Can't you even spell?"

"I'll answer that," said Jacob Two-Two, "I'll answer that, if you tell me how many times two goes into two?"

"Think I'm an idiot, do you? The answer to that," said The Hooded Fang, thrusting out his chest, "is one."

21

"And that," said Jacob Two-Two twice, "is how many suns we have."

"You're not playing fair! You're cheating."

"I am not! I am not!"

"All right, then, smarty-pants. Tell me how many ounces there are in a pound."

"Why, that's easy. That's easy," said Jacob Two-Two. "There are two times two times two times two ounces in a pound."

Shaking with rage, counting on his fingers, and then removing his shoes to use his toes as well, The Hooded Fang had to admit that Jacob Two-Two was right. "Oh, I hate you," he bellowed. "I could chew you up right here and now."

"But, Mr Hooded Fang," said Jacob Two-Two, "please, you mustn't be so sad."

"Mustn't I?"

"Because," said Jacob Two-Two, "you, too, can be a two-two."

"What's that, you little twerp?"

"How many sides are there to every story?" asked Jacob Two-Two. "How many sides are there to every story?"

"Two."

"What should every boy learn to stand on?"

"His own two feet."

"And what will it be when it gets dark?"

"Tonight."

"And where will you go tonight?"

"To bed."

"And what will it be when you wake up?"

"Why, tomorrow, of course," said The Hooded Fang, smiling just a little.

"You see, you see," exclaimed Jacob Two-Two, jumping up and down joyously, "It's easy, it's easy. You, too, are a two-two now."

The Hooded Fang's cheeks flared red. He looked like he was

going to explode. "All right, then. I've tried everything. And now there's only one thing to do. Tuesday afternoon at two o'clock, *I'm going to feed you to not* one, but two hungry sharks. Ho, ho!"

"Oh no," cried Jacob Two-Two. "Oh no."

"Oh yes," replied The Hooded Fang, "and what's more, I will personally bring you your last meal."

In most of the chapter from *Jacob Two-Two meets The Hooded Fang* on pages 20–23, the characters are talking to each other. If you read it aloud in groups of four, with one person as the storyteller and each of the other three playing a character, you could make it sound like a play. What clues can you find in the story to help you decide how to read your part? When you have had a chance to practise your reading, try it out on another group. You are the actors, and they are the audience.

Jacob ate some strange food while he was in prison. One menu that he had to choose from read:

THE PRISON MENU

CROCODILE STEAK
or
Tart of DEATH-WATCH BEETLE

ELECTRIC EEL SOUP
or
SNAKE BURGERS

NETTLE PIE

24

Make up a menu for Jacob's last meal before he is fed to two hungry sharks!

PICKING UP CLUES

.... IS THIS THE END OF JACOB TWO-TWO? .... What do you think?

Clever Jacob manages to make The Hooded Fang into a two-two person, by tricking him into saying a certain word. In twos, play the game where you win if you can make your partner say "Yes".

Who is your favourite "Baddie" character in a book?
   Describe him or her to the rest of the class. You could draw a "Wanted" poster, then write your description underneath. Put all your posters into a class exhibition called "Baddies in Books".
   Would the Hooded Fang be in your list of "Top Ten Baddies"?

IF AT FIRST YOU DO NOT SEE

A PICTURE RIDDLE - BOY OR BIRD?

Reading the pictures, poems and stories in this part of the book will help you to look at ideas and people in new ways.

Just imagine a boy changing into a bird. Here is how it happens!

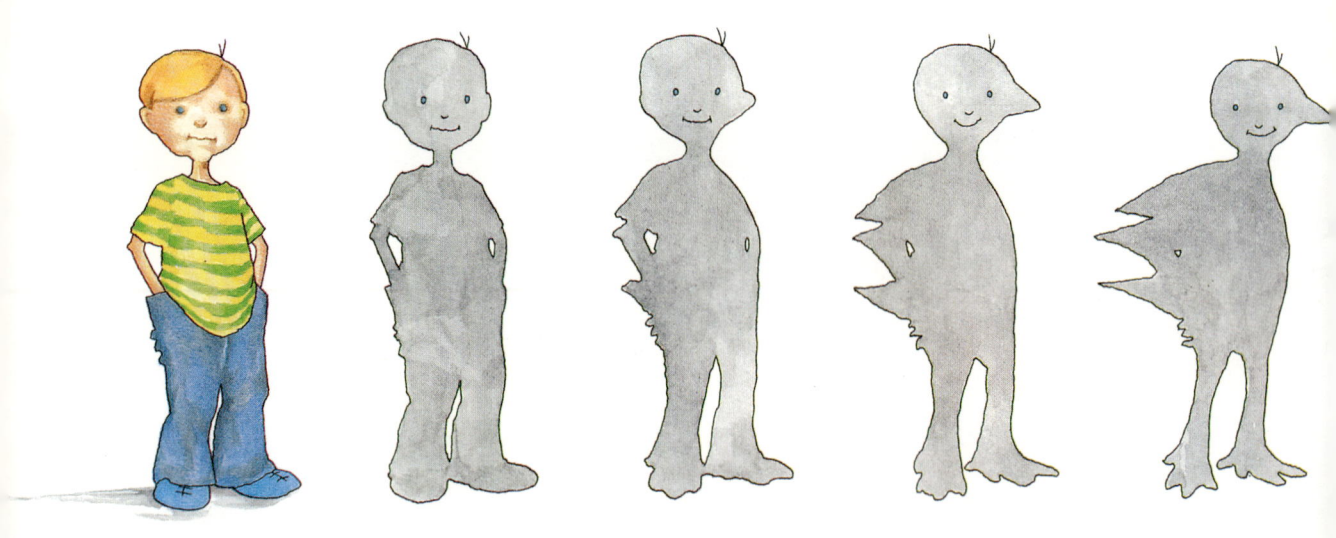

If you were a bird . . .

Look carefully at these pictures with a friend.

Make a list of all the changes which take place in the eight pictures which show the boy becoming a bird. Share your list with two other friends. Add to your own list any small points you missed the first time.

IF AT FIRST YOU DO NOT SEE

. . . you could fly . . .

Later in the story, the bird is frightened by a cat and decides to change into a dog.

Work with a friend. Copy the picture of the bird. See if you can change the bird into a dog in six drawings.

Share your "dog" with the rest of the class.

How many different kinds of "dogs" have you got? Which drawings do you think work best? Why?

WHAT'S IN A NAME?

Look carefully at the letter shapes. Notice how each one has been cleverly used to make a different part of the animals. Which drawing do you think works best?

Can you make the shape of another creature or object out of the letters of its name? It is not as easy as it looks.

You have seen how letter shapes can be used to make pictures. In this poem, names from a telephone directory have been used to make the sounds of a well-known nursery rhyme. Say the poem aloud, give it its usual name, then write it out the way it is normally written.

Humm Tee Dim Tay
Sato Nawol
Huntly Dumke
Hudd Agate Fall
Alder King Soss
Isan Dorley Kinsman
Coode Dant Pot
Humphrey Duhig Adda Arr Gaine

WHAT'S IN A SHAPE?

Now you've seen shapes made from letters, and a poem made from names. What about these? Are they pictures or poems?

A Moonshot falling

RING CLATTER ding dong PEAL CHIME

short it bursts in a shower of stars then reels down to distant trees an ember dying

Make a list of words to describe the *shapes*, *sounds* and *movements* of lots of different FIREWORKS.

Choose one firework to describe in a "shape poem".

Pick the best words from your list and arrange them into the shape of the firework.

You could give your poem an interesting "shape title".

Every poem has its own shape.
Read this sentence:

I saw a building soar into the sky making the sky's eye sore.

How would you write it out as a poem? Try lots of different ways before you decide which one you prefer.

Look on page 73 to see how the poet, Roger McGough, set it out. He had to think about the shape of the words on the page in the same way as you did. Do you prefer your way to his, or were they the same?

WHAT'S IN A POEM?

Poems are ...
... sometimes a surprise!

One poem which takes us by surprise is this one about the hairy, blood-stained thing.
It's by Roy Fuller.

In the bathroom

What is that blood-stained thing –
Hairy, as if it were frayed –
Stretching itself along
The slippery bath's steep side?

I approach it, ready to kill,
Or run away, aghast;
And find I have to deal
With a used elastoplast.

What "ordinary" things in the house have you been surprised by, even afraid of, when you first saw them – perhaps a crack in the ceiling; some old clothes hanging next to shoes in the wardrobe; a piece of string?

Write your own poem beginning with the words "What is that ...?"

Remember to keep your surprise until the last line.

Choose a title that will keep your secret.

Read your poem aloud.

How many of your friends guessed what the thing was before the end of your poem?

IF AT FIRST YOU DO NOT SEE

In this next poem by Roy Fuller, we are not told what the poet has seen, but we can guess if we listen to what he says as he sweeps the leaves. Read the poem several times, as if you were the poet thinking aloud. Remember that punctuation marks are there to help you with the meaning.

Autumn

Sweeping up leaves, I come
across a few dead blooms
I just don't remember
growing in summer – queer
pink-striped stalks; and some
purple cone shapes – mushrooms?
"Last week's Fifth November,"
I think, and all is clear.

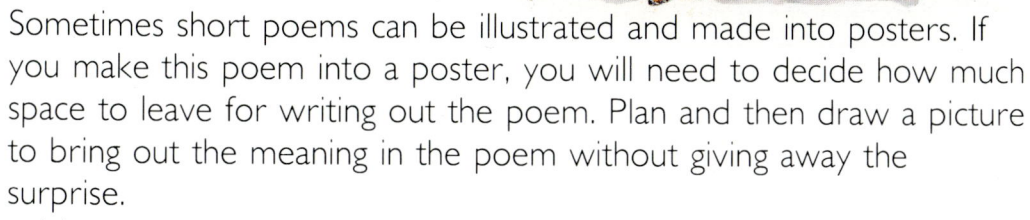

Sometimes short poems can be illustrated and made into posters. If you make this poem into a poster, you will need to decide how much space to leave for writing out the poem. Plan and then draw a picture to bring out the meaning in the poem without giving away the surprise.

You will find one example of a "poster poem" on page 73.

HODGEHEG

What have you just read at the top of the page?
Did you look again?
What did you expect to see?

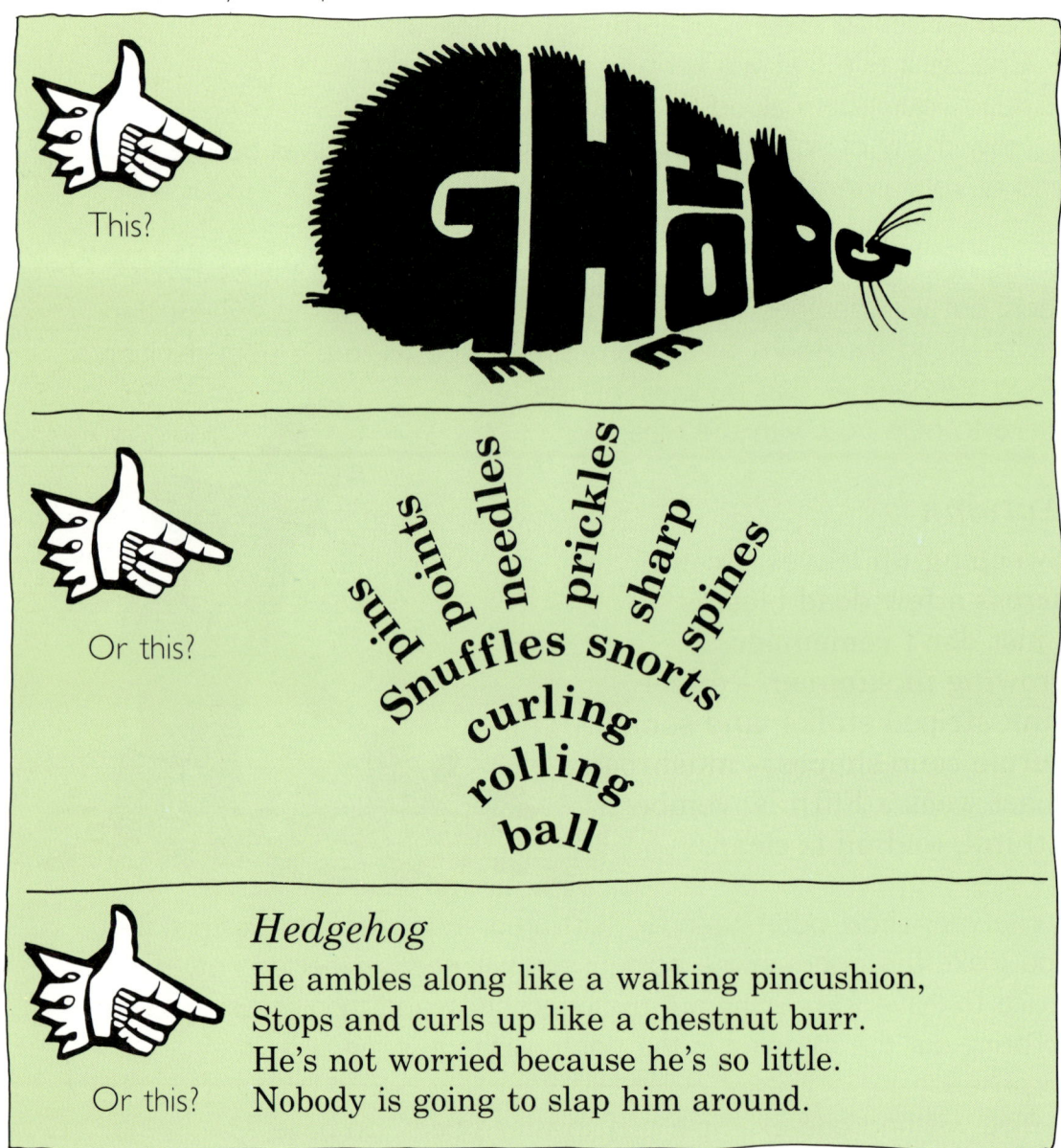

This?

Or this?

pins points needles prickles sharp spines
Snuffles snorts
curling
rolling
ball

Or this?

Hedgehog
He ambles along like a walking pincushion,
Stops and curls up like a chestnut burr.
He's not worried because he's so little.
Nobody is going to slap him around.

IF AT FIRST YOU DO NOT SEE

The Hodgeheg
DICK KING-SMITH

Bet it wasn't this!

If we take up the story on page 21 of this book by Dick King-Smith, you will be able to find out why Max thinks he is a hodgeheg!

    The family had crowded round him on his return, all talking at once.
    "Where have you been all this time?" asked Ma.
    "Are you all right, son?" asked Pa.
    "Did you cross the road?" they both said, and Peony, Pansy and Petunia echoed, "Did you? Did you? Did you?"
    For a while Max did not reply. His thoughts were muddled, and when he did speak, his words were muddled too.
    "I got a head on the bump," he said slowly.
    The family looked at one another.

"Something bot me on the hittom," said Max, "and then I headed my bang. My ache bads headly."

"But did you cross the road?" cried his sisters.

"Yes," said Max wearily. "I hound where the fumans cross over, but –"

"But the traffic only stops if you're a human?" interrupted Pa.

"Yes," said Max. "*Not* if you're a hodgeheg."

* * * * *

Max slept the clock round and half-way round again; he did not stir till the evening of the following day. The shock had sent him into a kind of short, early hibernation . . .

"How are you feeling, dear?" said Ma.

Max considered this. His headache was almost gone, and he was thinking straight, but his speech, he found, would still not behave properly.

"I'm a bet bitter, thanks," he said.

"You had a nasty knock," said Pa.

"You need rest," said Ma. "Why not get back into bed? We will bring you some nice slugs."

"I don't want to bed into get," said Max. "I feel quite wakeawide. In fact I feel like walking for a go."

Pa took a moment to work this one out. Then he said firmly, "You're not going anywhere, son, d'you hear me? You stay home in the garden for a while. Get your strength back, understand?"

"Yes, Pa," said Max. "I'll say what you do." And he did do what Pa had said, for a week or more.

In the rest of the book Max tries to find out how to cross the road safely.

He is puzzled by **"the black and white stripes; the red and green men and the big fuman in a white coat with the magic wand"**.

In small groups, pretend to be Hodgeheg's family. One of you should play the part of Hodgeheg. You have just returned from one of your adventures when you tried to **"hound out where fumans cross over the road"**.

Tell your family your story and answer any questions they ask you.

You could take it in turns to be Hodgeheg if several of you "bike talking lackwards"!

Look back to page 32.

Talk about all the different ways of looking at a hedgehog.

Can you find any other poems, pictures, stories and facts to add to this collection?

Do you know any other stories in which human beings are looked at from an animal's point of view? Tell your friends about them.

Make up a story in which an animal comes into your classroom and tries to understand what is going on.

IF AT FIRST YOU DO NOT SEE

GOING SPACES IS GOOD FOR YOU

Do you remember the book *Blue Misty Monsters*? (The cover is on page 12.) It's about a family from Outer Space who visit Earth.

Talk about what *you* think creatures from another planet might say about us if they visited Earth.

Write down your ideas under various headings. Here are some to start you off: Appearance; Food; Houses; Transport; Behaviour.

Now go into orbit and take a look at humans as the Blue Misty Monsters see us.

The Zome Kraft hissed through Outer Space and entered the solar system, left of the sun and right of the moon, where it altered course and began to slow down, spinning towards its destination.

"Commence Earth Approach!" ordered Mum Misty, crouching over the Control Panel.

"Commence Approach!" echoed Dad.

"Is that it?" asked Odle.

"What?"

"Earth," said Odle, and he bam-bam-bammed what he could see of it on the see-screen with his space gun.

"That's Earth," said Dad. "Stay away from those launch buttons, Odle!"

"I'm hungry!" little Mo announced.

"You're always hungry," said Odle.

IF AT FIRST YOU DO NOT SEE

"But I *am*," said Mo. "Isn't there anything to eat?"

"Zero 3900, descending," said Mum. "Give her a food block, somebody."

Dad gave Mo a food block. It was small, about the size of a chocolate bar, but it was packed with energy.

"Yummy!" said Mo, taking a big bite.

"I bet you'll be sick," said Odle.

"*You* make me sick!" said Mo.

"Not as sick as you'll be if an old Two-Legger Earth Monster gets you," said Odle.

"Odle!" snapped Mum and Dad Misty, together.

"Are there many Earth Monsters, Mum?" Mo asked, nervously.

"Lots!" said Odle. "There are Flappers that fly and Finners that swim and Roarers that roar in the jungle and horrible Two-Leggers and . . ."

"They're all very small, Mo dear," said Mum, quickly. "You *know* that."

"Will they eat me?" asked Mo, finishing the last bite of her food block.

"No," said Mum.

"Yes!" said Odle.

"ODLE!" said Dad.

"And spit out the pips," Odle added, cheerfully.

"Any more of that and I'll turn this Kraft round and go straight home, Odle," said Mum Misty, firmly. "No holiday. No going about to look at Earth Monsters. NOTHING! Understand?"

"Yes, Mum," said Odle, and he went back to bam-bam-bamming Earth.

"I want to go home," said Mo, climbing into her Pod, where she snuggled down in comfort.

"Zero 3500, descending," said Mum.

"Zero 3500, descending," confirmed Dad.

"Mo likes being at home," said Odle. "She doesn't enjoy Going Spaces."

"Going Spaces is good for you," said Mum. "It broadens the mind."

"What mind?" said Odle. "She hasn't got one!" He bounced over to Mo's Pod, and bam-bam-bammed what he could see of her.

"Odle!" said both of the big Mistys, angrily.

"Stay away from those launch buttons, Odle!" added Dad Misty. "How many more times must I tell you?"

"Sorry," said Odle.

"Don't say sorry unless you mean it," said Mum. "Entering Orbit."

"Entering Orbit," Dad repeated.

The Zome Kraft began to spin slowly round the earth. The lid of Mo's Pod slid back.

"What are *those*, Mum?" Mo asked, pointing at the big shapes on the see-screen. "Are they Monsters?"

"Those are Mountains, Mo. I've told you before. The Earth Monsters are small, even the Two-Leggers. They are titchy little things compared to us."

"They eat other Earth Monsters, Two-Leggers do," said Odle.

"I don't want to go to Earth," said Mo. "I wish we'd stayed at home."

"You'll have a Two-Legger disguise on, Mo," said Mum. "You'll be able to walk around Earth and the Two-Leggers won't know you're not one of them."

"I don't want to look like them" said Mo. "They're stupid, and ugly."

"Don't be silly, Mo," said Mum.

"Those are houses, just below us," said Dad, hurriedly changing the subject.

"What are *houses*, Dad?" asked Odle, peering at them.

"Two-Legger Dwellings, Odle," said Dad. "The things they live in."

"Why do they live packed close together, like that?" asked Odle, peering at the see-screen. "All squashed up tight against each other?"

"They don't know any better," said Mum.

"They're not very bright," said Dad.

"I want to go home," said Mo, in a sulky voice. She climbed

IF AT FIRST YOU DO NOT SEE

inside her Pod again, and slid the door closed over her head.

"Bam!" shouted Odle, dancing round Mo's Pod, and making faces at her. "Bam-bam-bam-bam! Scared of old Two-Leggers! Scaredy Mo! Bam-bam-bam-b-a-a-a-m!"

The b-a-a-a-m was his undoing, for he tripped, and fell on top of the launch buttons.

ZOOOOOOOM!

One moment Mo's Pod was there, with Mo in it, and the next it wasn't.

"Mo!" Mum screamed. Mo was gone, powering ahead of the Zome Kraft with her Pod Boosters ablaze. There was nothing Mum and Dad could do to stop her descent to Earth, and nothing poor Mo could do either, because she was too small to know how her Pod worked.

Down, down, down the Pod sped, down down down to . . .

. . . the garden at the back of Number 73 Edgeword Street, where Spud lived with his Mum and Dad.

The beginning of this story could easily become a very good playscript for you to read aloud. We have begun to write it; you finish writing it. You can read it aloud in groups of five.

Look out below! (A play for voices)

(sound effects of spacecraft hissing through space)
Storyteller: The Zome Kraft hissed through Outer Space and entered the solar system, left of the sun and right of the moon, where it altered course and began to slow down, spinning towards its destination.
Mum: Commence Earth Approach!
Dad: Commence Approach!
Odle: Is that it?
Dad: What?
Odle: Earth.
Dad: That's Earth. Stay away from those launch buttons. Odle!
Mo: I'm hungry!
Odle: You're always hungry!
Mo: But I AM . . . . Isn't there anything to eat?
Mum: Zero 3900, descending. Give her a food block, somebody . . . .

Now think about Spud. Make up some facts about him and write them down. What does he look like? How old is he? Has he any brothers or sisters? What hobbies is he interested in? Does he believe in creatures from Outer Space?

Now that you have some notes about Spud, imagine his first meeting with Mo. Think of some of the things he might tell her and ask her. It happened like this:

Spud was in the garden checking the fireworks ready for Guy Fawkes Night. That was when he first saw a blue mist coming towards him . . . .

Continue to write the story of their first meeting.

IF AT FIRST YOU DO NOT SEE

GOING PLACES IS GOOD FOR YOU

Reading a story is like going on a voyage of discovery without moving from the book corner.

If you travel with Panda on his journey, you might make some important discoveries, just as he did.

For many months he sailed about the world, asking his questions in ancient timeless places.

"Best not to worry," said the leopard. "You cannot change your spots."

"Shsssssh!" hissed the snake, "I change my entire outfit."

"Some of us are just born superior," said the cow in a holier-than-thou voice.

IF AT FIRST YOU DO NOT SEE

In small groups, think and talk about the answers given by the leopard, the snake, the cow and the chameleon. Try to guess what Panda's question was.

"It's all a matter of background," said the chameleon.

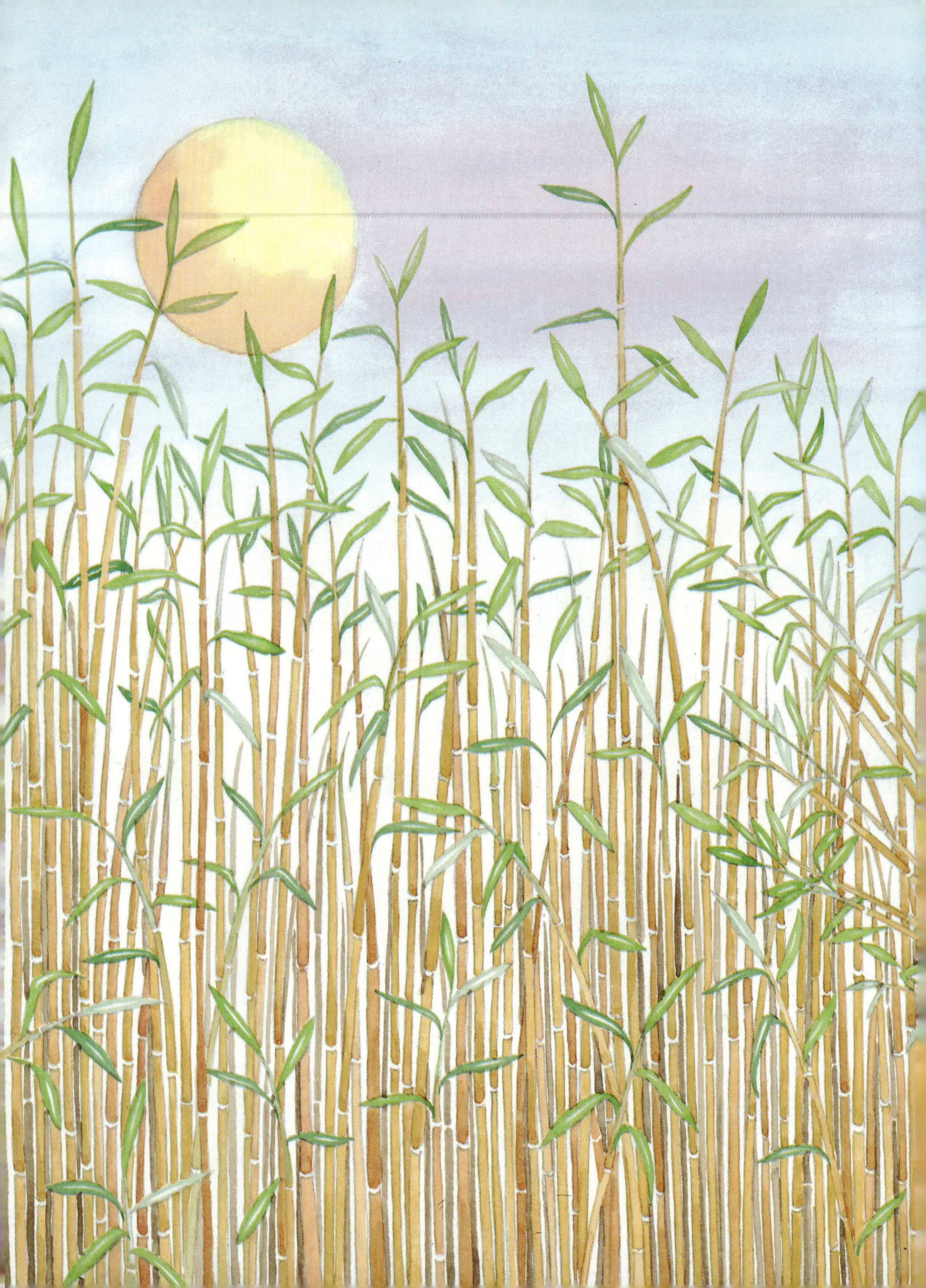

Write down all the questions you think of in your group. Decide which of them might be important enough to make Panda travel about the world to find an answer.

Did you guess what was puzzling Panda? The answer is on the back cover of the upside-down book:

What do you think about the answers Panda was given, and the characters of the creatures who gave them?

Imagine that Panda meets an ostrich and an eagle on his journey. Talk about what you already know about both these birds. What different answers might each give to Panda's question? In groups of three, act out the conversations they might have with Panda about his puzzle.

At the end of the journey, when Panda was asked **"But are you a black bear or a white bear?"** he replied, "I don't care!".

What do you think Panda had learned from going places, meeting "people" and asking questions?

IF AT FIRST YOU DO NOT SEE

Panda's Puzzle

"Am I a white bear with black bits or a black bear with white bits?" Panda travels through China, Egypt, the United States, the Himalayas and the Far East trying to resolve his puzzle. How can he find the answer and what will it reveal?

A PICTURE BOOK FOR ALL CHILDREN, ESPECIALLY SUITABLE FOR YOUNG READERS.

methuen moonlight

UK £1.50   0 90714 48 9

STORY TALK

THERE'S NOTHING TO DO - I'M BORED

Have you ever been irritated by someone asking questions?

Are there any sayings, such as the one at the top of this page or the ones below, which irritate you? Make a list.

> Everyone else has one.

> It's not fair.

> I'll do it in a minute.

Do adults have any sayings that get on your nerves?

Are there any sayings in the poem by David Jackson on page 47 that make you mad?

Can you add any more?

Irritating sayings

STORY TALK

    Isn't it time you thought about bed?
      It must be somewhere
    You speak to him, Harold, he won't listen to me.
      Who do you think I am?
    You'd better ask your father
      It's late enough as it is
    Don't eat with your mouth open
      In this day and age
    Did anybody ask your opinion
  I remember when I was a boy
And after all we do for you
  You're not talking to your school friends now you know
Why don't you do it the proper way
  I'm only trying to tell you
What did I just say
  Now, wrap up warm
B.E.D. spells bed
  Sit up straight and don't gobble your food
For the five hundredth time
  Don't let me ever see you do that again.
Have you made your bed?
      Can't you look further than your nose?
    No more lip
      Have you done your homework?
    Because I say so.
      Don't come those fancy ways here
    Any more and you'll be in bed
      My, haven't you grown
    Some day I won't be here, then you'll see
      A chair's for sitting on
    You shouldn't need telling at your age.
      Want, want, want, that's all you ever say

Michael Rosen has made many poems out of everyday sayings which he remembers from his own childhood. Here is one of them:

Shut your mouth when you're eating.
   I am, dad.
MOUTH!
   It *is* shut
I can see it isn't. I
can *hear* it isn't.
   What about *his*
   mouth? You can see
   everything in his
   mouth.
He's only two. He doesn't know any better.
   You can see all his peas and tomato sauce.
That's none of your business.

(2 minutes go by)

   Dad.
Yes.
   Your mouth's open. Shut your
   mouth when you're eating.
It is shut, thank you very much.
   I can see it isn't, Dad.

I can see all the food in there.
Look, that's my business, OK?
Peas, gravy, spuds, everything.
Look, you don't want to grow up to be as horrible as your father do you? Answer that, smartyboots.

Take one saying from your own list to make a "conversation poem".
Have a look at the poem, "Amanda", on pages 70–71 to give you another idea.
Read your poems in pairs.

A STORY...MAN!

Are there any sayings that you like hearing over and over again?

The poet John Agard remembers some of the proverbs that wise old Caribbean grannies used to say to children. We asked him to tell you a little about his granny.

"I grew up in Guyana, and when my mother was out at work, I spent a lot of time as a little boy with my grandmother. For children in the Caribbean, Granny is a very special person. When you fall and bump your head you run to Granny. When your mum picks up the belt to give you licks, you run to Granny. And you like to visit Granny because you know she keeps fudge and sugar-cake in her old biscuit tin just like she would keep your secrets. But Granny would sometimes tell you that if you don't hear when your mum speaks, then Granny can't always save you from licks. My own grandmother used to say, "Boy who don't hear, must feel". But many other grandmothers around the Caribbean have said that at some time. So in *Say it again, Granny* I've made up a granny from my own granny and bits of other boys' and girls' grannies."

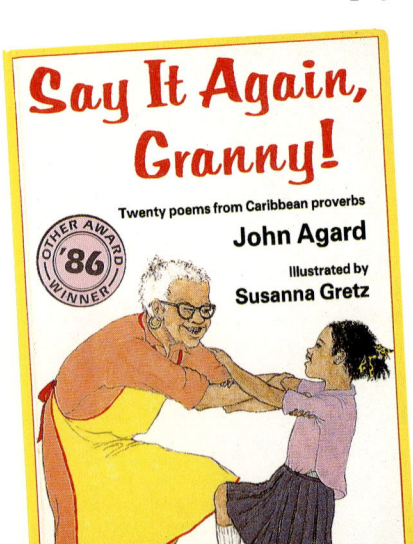

Here is one of John Agard's "proverb poems". If you have ever been late for school, you will enjoy reading it.

STORY TALK

Early bird does catch the fattest worm

Late again
going to be late again
for school again
and I can't say
I overslept
can't blame it
on the bus
can't blame it
on the train
can't blame it
on the rain
and Granny words
buzzing in my brain
"Early bird does catch the worm,"
and I thinking
Teacher going tell me off
and I wishing
I was a bird
and teacher was a juicy worm.

In pairs read aloud some of these sayings which John Agard has used in his poems. Do you recognise any of them?

Write down the words of any other sayings you know which have the same meanings as these:

Don't count your chickens before they hatch.
Who the cap fit, let them wear it.
No rain, no rainbow.
Bad dancer mustn't blame the floor.
The older the violin the sweeter the tune.
Hurry-hurry mek bad curry.
When boss away, Jackass take holiday.
One finger can't catch flea.

Choose one of the sayings. Make up a story about a young child and a granny. Finish your story with the words of the saying you have chosen.

Games with marbles are played by children all over the world. In Guyana they call one game "Three-hole". John Agard writes about it in this poem:

Three-hole
is the name
of a marble game
we got in Guyana.

Is fun to play
and not hard.
Just dig three lil holes
in you yard
or the sand
by you gate.

Then aim straight

for first-hole
   second-hole
      third-hole.

If you lucky
and you marble
go in all the holes
one two three

Then is you chance
to knock you friend marble.
Send it flying for a dance.
When marble burst then fun start

With a friend, read the poem to find out how to play the game.

Talk about any other marble games you know. Write a poem about a playground game you enjoy.
   Here is an idea to get you thinking:

Hopscotch
is the name
of a playground game
we got in our school.

Draw a picture to go with your poem.

TALK IN STORIES

You will probably know lots of stories in which animals talk and behave like human beings. Stories like these are called fables. From them we can learn something new about ourselves and other people. You could say that *Panda's puzzle* on pages 42–45 is a modern fable. This one is an Indian tale which was first told a long time ago.

Hare heralds the earthquake

There was once a hare who was always worrying: "Oh dear," he muttered all day long, "oh deary, deary me."

His greatest worry was that there might be an earthquake. "For if there was," said he to himself, "whatever would become of me?"

He was feeling particularly anxious about this one morning, when suddenly an enormous fruit fell down from a nearby tree – *CRASH!!* – making the whole earth shake.

At once the hare leaped up.

"It's happened! The earthquake's come!"

And with that, he ran madly off.

He raced across the fields, where many of his cousins were feeding.

"Help, help, there's been an earthquake! Quickly – run for your lives!"

STORY TALK

So all the hares left the fields and madly began to follow.

They raced across the plains, through forests and rivers and into the hills where many other cousins were sleeping.

"Help, help, the earthquake's coming! As quick as you can you must flee!"

So all the hares left the rivers and plains, the hills and forests and madly began to follow.

"An earthquake? How dreadful! Whatever shall we do?"

By the time they reached the mountains, there were ten thousand hares altogether, pounding like thunder up the slopes.

Soon they reached the highest peak. The first hare gazed back to see if the earthquake was coming any closer, but all he could see was a great swarm of animals speeding along behind.

Then he looked in front in case the earthquake had sneaked round a corner and was waiting to catch them ahead. But all he could see was more mountains and valleys and, far in the distance, the shining blue of the sea.

As he stood there panting, a new animal came along, a lion.

"What is happening?" asked he.

"Earthquake, earthquake!" babbled all the hares.

The lion's mane waved gently in the breeze.

"An earthquake? Who has seen it? Who has heard it?"

"Ask him, ask him!" cried all the hares, pointing their paws at the first one.

The lion turned to him and waited.

"Please sir," said the hare shyly, "I was sitting quietly at home when there was this terrible crash and the ground shook and I knew it must be a 'quake, sir, so I got out fast as I could and warned all the others to save their lives."

The lion looked at the hare from his deep, wise eyes.

"My brother, would you be brave enough to show me where this dreadful disaster happened?"

The hare didn't really feel brave enough at all, but there was something about the lion which he felt he ought to trust.

So, rather timidly, he led him back down the mountains and the hills, across the rivers, plains, forests and fields, until at last they were back at his home.

"This is where I heard it, sir."

The lion gazed around; and very soon he spotted the enormous fruit which had fallen so noisily from its tree.

He picked it up in his mouth, climbed onto a rock and dropped it back to the ground.

CRASH!!

The hare jumped. "Oh sir, help! Earthquake! Quickly – get away – it's just happened again!"

But suddenly he realised that the lion was laughing. And then he saw the fruit rocking gently beside his feet.

"Oh," he whispered, "it wasn't really an earthquake after all . . .?"

"No," said the lion, "it was not indeed and you had no need to be afraid."

"What a *silly* hare I've been!"

The lion smiled kindly. "Never mind, little brother. All of us – even I – sometimes fear things we cannot understand."

And with that he padded back to the ten thousand hares that were still waiting on top of the mountain, to tell them that it was now quite safe to go home.

In small groups, talk about the story.

Can you tell from his conversation what kind of "person" the hare is?

What do we learn about the lion from what he says?

What do you think the hare learned from this experience? Write down the sentence from the story which tells us this.

Tell a story about a time when you were afraid because you did not understand what was happening.

If you decide to write your story, think carefully how to use talk. You should use it:

- to say important things;
- to make your story more interesting and exciting;
- to help the reader to understand your feelings.

Remember to begin a new line every time someone begins to speak.

STORIES IN QUILTS

Have you ever thought that there could be stories in quilts? The book, *The patchwork quilt*, by Valerie Flourney, is all about a family and their very special quilt.

"A quilt won't forget. It can tell your life story," said Tanya's Grandma. As the children grew out of favourite clothes and celebrated special times, the old lady cut out pieces of leftover scraps and added them to the quilt she was making.

When Grandma became too ill to go on stitching, the three grandchildren carried on adding their "stories" to the quilt.

Tanya remembered to take some squares from her Grandma's old quilt so that Grandma too would be part of the new one.

Finally the day came when the work was almost done and Grandma was well enough to add the finishing touches.

Nobody realized how big the quilt had grown, or how beautiful it was. Reds, greens, blues and golds, light colours and dark, blended in and out throughout the quilt.

"It's beautiful," Papa said. He touched the gold patch, looked at Mama and remembered. Jim remembered too – there was his blue and the red from Ted's shirt. There was Tanya's African princess costume. And there was Grandma. And even though her patch was old, it fitted perfectly with the rest.

They all remembered the past year. They especially

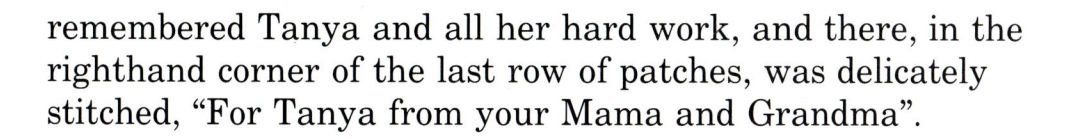

remembered Tanya and all her hard work, and there, in the righthand corner of the last row of patches, was delicately stitched, "For Tanya from your Mama and Grandma".

At one point in this story Tanya said:

"Grandma isn't lonely, she and the quilt are telling each other stories."

Talk about what you think she meant.

Bring any of your favourite patches into school. What stories do they tell? Share them with your friends. Use all of your patches to make a class story quilt.

STORY TALK

Leonard Clark tells his quilt story in a poem.

On one visit to his grandmother who is ill in bed, he remembers seeing ...

The quilt

Her patchwork quilt,
A huge and dangling square,
Triangles of white, oblongs of red,
With bits from curtain and kilt.
I thought it looked just like
A landscape of little fields, seen
In springtime from an aeroplane,
Or, with dots of orange-green,
The mottled back of some big river pike.
And there were strips of calico in that counterpane,
Flannel from a grey Welsh shirt,
A blue velvet diamond, some sprigged lawn,
Faded pieces of a gingham skirt.
And as we slowly watched the dawn
Chequering the vast and empty sky,
"That was my wedding dress" she softly said,
Placing her fingers on one silky hexagon; ...

AND BEDSPREADS

Amelia and Maud were two old sisters who lived at opposite ends of a long bed. They agreed with each other about only one thing – the white bedspread that covered their long bed was boring. So each decided to embroider her own end of the bedspread with a picture of the house they had lived in when they were children.

They began at the front door:

Maud cut a neat oblong of purple velvet for her door, and worked each panel in fine spider stitch. She made the railings of hairpin lace, and crocheted a half-moon for the fanlight over the door.

Amelia made her door from the pocket of an old blue dress, and cut the steps out of a pair of old fawn knickers.

She found a brass button for the doorknob, a buckle for the letterbox, and a curtain ring for the knocker. And as she couldn't remember any of her stitches, she had to invent them as she went along.

Each day they added more to their houses until on Saturday all that remained to do was the garden.

Maud worked a pretty border of flowers in raised satin stitch. But Amelia's garden was like a jungle, with trees to climb, and a swing in the apple tree.

62

On Sunday they turned the bedspread round so that they could see each other's houses.

When they were about a hundred and three years old, the sisters died and their bedspread was put in a museum for all to see . . .

Here is a picture of the door that Maud embroidered:

Can you draw Amelia's door by following closely the description of it on page 61?

Look at the finished bedspread.
　　Talk about the differences between the two pictures of the house and garden.
　　Can you guess which sister embroidered the sun?
　　Why do you think the houses and gardens look so different when the sisters were both remembering the same house?
　　If you read *The bedspread* by Sylvia Fair, you'll find out how all the different bits of the bedspread were made.

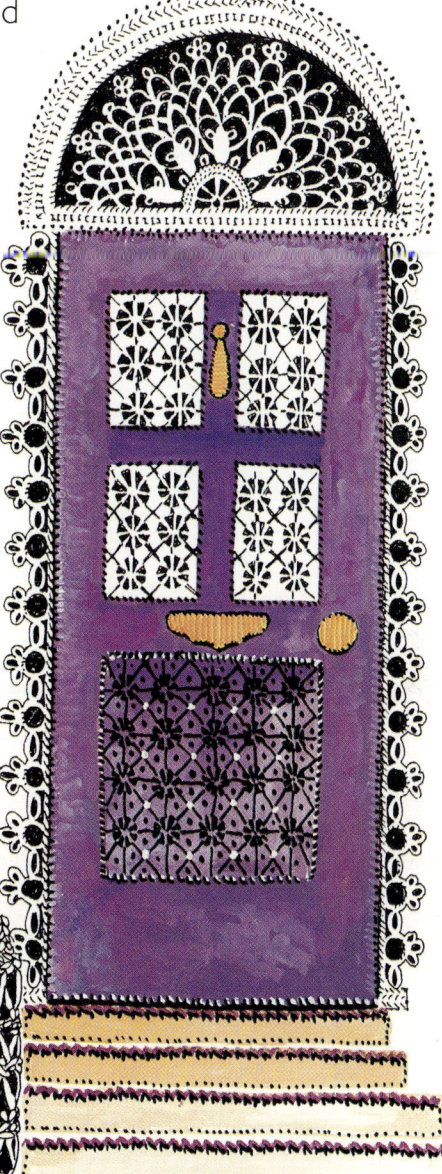

STORY TALK

AND EVEN WALLPAPER

Helen Ganly looked at rolls of wallpaper and saw a story!
   The story she tells, *Jyoti's journey*, is about an eight-year-old Indian girl called Jyoti. Here she is:

This is Jyoti. She is eight years old. She was born in a village in India.

We learn interesting things about Jyoti's life and the celebration of a family wedding. One day Jyoti's father sends a letter saying that he has saved up enough money for her and her mother to join him in England.

Finally the day came when mother and Jyoti said goodbye. Grandmother, the baby and the little sisters were going to stay with an auntie and uncle in the village.

A beautiful white aeroplane sped through the night, taking them to far away England.

Collect materials such as wallpaper, felt and wool, and make a picture of what Jyoti would see if she came to your school, home or street. Your picture could show a park you know, or a family celebration such as a birthday or wedding, or Christmas.

Write a few sentences to go under your picture so that Jyoti can learn something about her new country.

If stories can come out of quilts, bedspreads and wallpaper, you should be able to think of other things that have a story to tell. What about letters, coins, photographs, shoes and toys, for example?

Look for something interesting to bring to school that has a story you would like to share with the others in your class.

Find out all you can about the object, where it came from, who made it ... and why it is important to you.

DROP EVERYTHING AND READ

RAMONA QUIMBY, AGED EIGHT

In this book we have talked a great deal about WHAT and HOW to read. Let's now think about WHERE and WHEN we most enjoy reading.

Many people read in bed; on the floor; curled up in a comfortable chair; in the bath; on the train . . . .

Where is your favourite reading place?

You may be lucky and have an attractive corner of the classroom, cosy with cushions and carpet and full of inviting books.

Ramona Quimby did not have a book corner in her classroom. But still the best part of the day was "SSR".

Just before her class was to make its weekly visit to the school library, Mrs Whaley announced, "Today and from now on we are going to have Sustained Silent Reading every day."

Ramona liked the sound of Sustained Silent Reading, even though she was not sure what it meant, because it sounded important.

Mrs Whaley continued, "This means that every day after lunch we are going to sit at our desks and read silently to ourselves any book we choose in the library."

"Even mysteries?" someone asked.

"Even mysteries," said Mrs Whaley.

"Do we have to give book reports on what we read?" asked one suspicious member of the class.

"No book reports on your Sustained Silent Reading books," Mrs Whaley promised the class. Then she went on, "I don't think Sustained Silent Reading sounds very interesting, so I think we will call it something else." Here she printed four big letters on the blackboard, and as she pointed she read out, "D – E – A – R. Can anyone guess what these letters stand for?"

The class thought and thought.

"Do Everything All Right," suggested someone. A good thought, but not the right answer.

"Don't Eat A Reader," suggested Yard Ape. Mrs Whaley laughed and told him to try again.

DROP EVERYTHING AND READ

As Ramona thought, she stared out the window at the blue sky, the treetops, and, in the distance, the snow-capped peak of Mount Hood looking like a giant licked ice-cream cone. *R* could stand for Run and *A* for And. "Drop Everything And Run," Ramona burst out. Mrs Whaley, who was not the sort of teacher who expected everyone to raise a hand before speaking, laughed and said, "Almost right, Ramona, but have you forgotten we are talking about reading?"

"Drop Everything And Read!" chorused the rest of the class. Ramona felt silly. She should have thought of that herself.

Ramona decided that she preferred Sustained Silent Reading to DEAR because it sounded more grown-up. When time came for everyone to Drop Everything And Read, she sat quietly doing her Sustained Silent Reading.

How peaceful it was to be left alone in school. She could read without trying to hide her book under her desk or behind a bigger book. She was not expected to write lists of words she did not know, so she could figure them out by skipping and guessing. Mrs Whaley did not expect the class to write summaries of what they read either, so she did not have to choose easy books to make sure she would get her summary right. Now if Mrs Whaley would leave her alone to draw, too, school would be almost perfect.

Yes, Sustained Silent Reading was the best part of the day.

AMANDA

Have you ever been "told off" for reading – a comic under the desk, with a torch under the bedclothes, or when you should have been doing something else?

Do you think Amanda sounds like the sort of girl who would like to shut out nagging adults by hiding behind a book? Try reading this poem by Robin Klein in pairs. One of you can be the grown-up, and the other one Amanda.

Don't bite your nails, Amanda!
Don't hunch your shoulders, Amanda!
Stop that slouching and sit up straight, Amanda!

(There is a languid, emerald sea,
where the sole inhabitant is me –
a mermaid, drifting blissfully.)

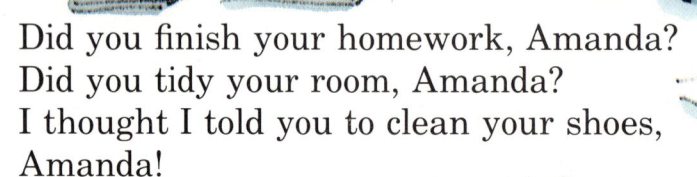

Did you finish your homework, Amanda?
Did you tidy your room, Amanda?
I thought I told you to clean your shoes, Amanda!

(I am an orphan, roaming the street.
I pattern soft dust with my hushed, bare feet.
The silence is golden, the freedom is sweet.)

NAG! NAG!

Don't eat that chocolate, Amanda!
Remember your acne, Amanda!
Will you please look at me when I'm speaking to you,
Amanda!

(I am Rapunzel, I have not a care;
life in a tower is tranquil and rare;
I'll certainly *never* let down my bright hair!)

NAG! NAG!

Stop that sulking at once, Amanda!
You're always so moody, Amanda!
Anyone would think that I nagged at you,

Amanda!

DROP EVERYTHING AND READ

LONG LEGS OR LONG EARS?

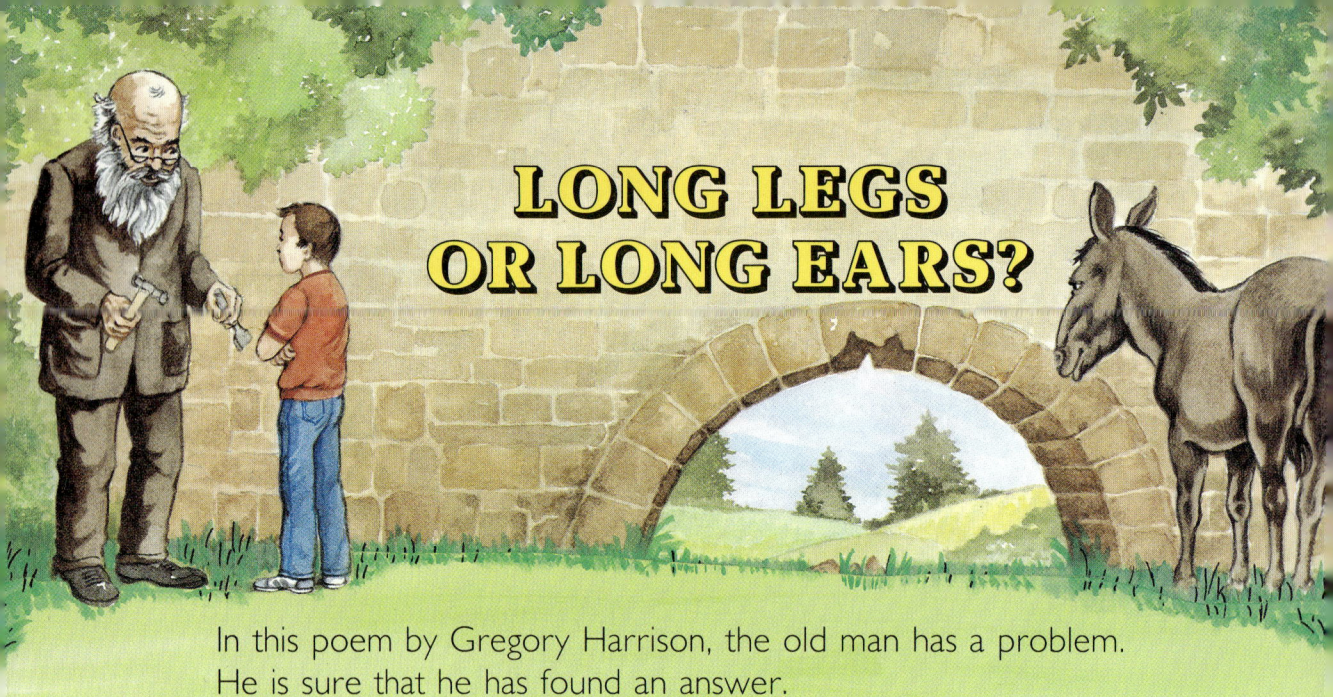

In this poem by Gregory Harrison, the old man has a problem.
He is sure that he has found an answer.
 A boy comes along, sees the problem and has another idea.
 Can you think of any other answers?

"Are you pleased with the donkey you bought at the fair?"
I asked the old man with the flowing white hair.
"Oh yes, a fine beast. I've had him since March.
But that bridge is a nuisance.
His ears catch on the arch.
So,
I'm cutting some grooves for his ears in the stone,
But it takes a long time
When you're working alone."

"It's none of my business," I said with a smile,
"But I had it in mind that it might be worth while
To dig out the path –
Less work don't you know."

He thought for a minute and then answered slow,
"Ah, yes, but hold on, it's not how it appears;
He ain't long in the leg;
He's too long in the ears."

A POSTER POEM

DROP EVERYTHING AND READ

Eye sore

I saw
a building
soar
into the sky

making
the sky's
eye
sore.

A HAMSTER AT LARGE

Read what some children said about this story after they had heard it.

Very, very very, very very... good.

Good – it could be about me.

I can bring home the school rabbit.

I'm glad the burglary happened. A dog is a much better pet than a hamster.

Imagine having nine babies.

Mothers can be very sensible sometimes.

In pairs talk about what you think the story is about. Jot down your thoughts.

Listen to the story or read it to each other. It's from *The Elm Street lot*, by Philippa Pearce.

In the beginning there were no hamsters in Elm Street at all. Plenty of other pets, of course: dogs, cats, budgerigars, tortoises, and so on. Every one of the Elm Street lot had a pet, even if it was only Jimmy Clegg's caterpillar.

Everyone except Ginger Jones. . . .

Ginger longed for a pet, but his mother always said the same thing: "I have a husband and a son, both bringing dirt into the house and needing constant attention, day in, day out, week after week. I don't want another creature." So no dog or cat or anything else for Ginger Jones.

"What about a hamster?" Sim Tolland had once said to

Ginger. For although nobody in Elm Street owned a hamster, everyone knew they weren't much trouble, because Woodside School always has a hamster. It's part of their Nature.

Ginger shook his head helplessly. "Day in, day out," he quoted, "week after week, month after month, year after . . ."

Then Sim Tolland had his brain wave. You see, the Woodside hamster can never stay in the school in holiday-time – there's no one regularly to look after her. (This particular hamster was a female, called Elaine, after the school cook.) So, in holiday-time, one of the children – a different one each time – takes her home and looks after her until term starts again. Sim's brain wave was that Ginger Jones should take Elaine home. His mother couldn't object to a *temporary* hamster; and the idea was that Elaine would give Mrs Jones a taste, so to speak, of hamsters. A nice taste, of course. She'd see what pretty, clean creatures they are. How little they eat. How little room a hamster's cage takes up; and so on.

Careful preparations were needed at Woodside. To begin with, every one of the Elm Street lot swore an oath not to offer, against Ginger, to take Elaine. As for children from other streets – they had to be persuaded to keep their mouths shut and their hands down when the teacher asked for a volunteer. You could offer them marbles or chewing-gum or iced lollies or peanuts, or you could offer to make them into mincemeat.

This part of the plan went well. At the end of term Miss Borwich said: "Well, now, who wants Elaine this time?"

Absolute silence; absolute stillness. One or two of the children went pale with the strain; and somebody poked Ginger to wake him up. But he wasn't day-dreaming; just temporarily dazed. It had been arranged that he should speak up in a loud, clear, trustworthy voice; but all that came out was a creaky whisper: "Me. I'll take her."

"No one else offering?" Miss Borwich said in surprise. She looked round at everybody, and everybody stared back at her, willing her to hand Elaine over to Ginger. She looked at Ginger, and he managed a trustworthy smile.

"Well," Miss Borwich said uneasily, "if Herbert Jones is the only one to volunteer –"

"He is," said Sim Tolland. . . .

So Ginger took Elaine home.

Now Elaine really was a beauty – Ginger said she could have been a beauty queen. She was nearly as big as half a pound of butter, and in parts not far off the same colour. She had bright little black eyes – only Mrs Jones called them beady – and she had a nice character. Quite soon Ginger taught her to run up his arm on to his shoulder and then, standing on her hind legs, to reach for some favourite food – a sunflower seed or a cornflake – which he had lodged behind his ear. There was a little exercise-wheel in Elaine's cage, and every evening she would get on to it and pedal it round: *creak! creak! creak!* Mr Jones said the sound got on his nerves . . . .

Ginger decided to make [Elaine] a bigger, grander cage than the school one. He knew what he was doing, and the new cage, when it was finished, was fit for a princess, with all kinds of little improvements. One thing turned out to be not an improvement: Ginger backed the cage with wood, without wire-mesh reinforcement. Soft wood, too; and in the night Elaine gnawed a hole right through it and escaped. Disappeared.

Ginger was very much upset, and so was his mother. Ginger thought that Elaine might starve; and Mrs Jones said, on the contrary, she couldn't bear the idea of that hamster running loose in the house and *fingering* everything eatable. She also said she lay awake at night hearing Elaine climbing up the legs of the bed.

Ginger's father said nothing . . . .

DROP EVERYTHING AND READ

That Sunday morning, early, there was a commotion from the house next door to the Joneses', where the Cleggs live. The Cleggs' front door was flung open and Mrs Clegg rushed out into the street. She was holding an opened cornflake packet in her hand, and she seemed to be shaking the packet wildly, and screaming. It was just as if she were getting an electric shock from the packet, but couldn't break the contact and get rid of the thing. It turned out that the cornflake packet was being shaken *from the inside*; not by Mrs Clegg at all. When Mrs Clegg recovered enough presence of mind to throw the packet from her, skimming it along the street, out popped Elaine. Out she popped, and under Sim Tolland's big brother's second-hand car, covered with plastic sheeting.

With Mrs Clegg having hysterics in the middle of Elm Street, everyone got to know what was going on. In a matter of seconds Ginger Jones and the rest of the Elm Street lot were on their hands and knees, peering under the car.

"I can see her!" said Ginger.

"If you mean that yellowish thing," said Sim Tolland, "it looks more like an old banana skin to me."

"I'd know her anywhere," said Ginger. "It's her."

"Whatever it is," said someone else, "it's not moving."

"She's petrified with fright," said Ginger. "We shall have to move the car to get her."

They had to move Mrs Clegg first, who was still laughing and sobbing about the packet of cornflakes. Then, having got the car key, they opened the door, took off the brake, and pushed the car out of its old position . . . .

When they'd got the car away, they found that the yellowish blur was an old curled up banana skin; and they noticed a kind of over-hang to the kerb of the pavement there, and Elaine must have run along under that – right away, and heaven knew where she was now.

For several days there was no sign whatsoever of Elaine. (It turned out later that she must have wandered away into one of the other streets whose gardens or yards back on to Elm Street.) Ginger was very low-spirited indeed. He said that he knew in his bones that one of the Elm Street cats had mistaken Elaine for a mouse, and eaten her.

Then, after several days, people in Elm Street began to complain of odd noises . . . hamster-hoards of food were found . . . Elaine was back.

Hamsters like travelling, especially by tunnel, and it can't have been too difficult in the terrace houses of Elm Street, especially with lofts whose partition walls are old and sometimes in bad condition. Elaine was seen only twice in the next few weeks. Once was by old Mr Crackenthorpe, when he was attending to the water-tank in his roof. He saw her and shouted at her: "You get out, or I'll boil you for my tea!" Elaine did get out.

And then Ginger saw her. He was at the elm stump by himself and very melancholy. Everyone else had gone off to the Park, but he simply hadn't the heart for it. . . .

It was very quiet, and Ginger was leaning sadly against the stump without moving. And then, with his downcast eyes, he saw Elaine – saw her come creeping out of the tree stump itself, between his very feet. He held his breath and watched her; she collected several . . . pieces of popcorn in her cheek pouches and then slipped back by the way she had come.

He stooped to examine the bottom of the tree stump. There was a hole that must be Elaine's front-doorway. It was big enough for Ginger to get two fingers in – and then Elaine bit them. But they had been in long enough to touch more than Elaine: she had babies with her. That's why it's certain that she had spent some time out of Elm Street, where there were no other hamsters, and somewhere else met a male hamster also on the run, and mated with him.

Now she had babies – there were nine of them. Ginger,

with Sim Tolland, managed to get the whole family out of the stump and back into the old cage. The cage was then kept in the Tollands' house. When the babies were old enough, Ginger and Sim gave them away, up and down Elm Street, and what with those hamsters and their descendants, there are always hamsters in Elm Street nowadays.

As for Elaine, Ginger took her back to Woodside at the end of the holidays. Miss Borwich, when she heard about the babies, said that she hoped the experience would be a warning to Elaine.

And Ginger? It would have been nice to have ended the story with Ginger's mother welcoming one of Elaine's babies into their home; but Mrs Jones said another hamster would enter the house only over her dead body.

So Ginger would have ended as he began, without a pet, if it hadn't been for the burglary. Burglars broke into the Joneses' house one Saturday afternoon when everyone was out. They didn't take anything much, but they made a mess of everything, and Mrs Jones was very, very much upset.... She put a notice on the gate saying, "Beware of the dog", and she hung a dog's lead and muzzle in the hall, where anyone could see who looked through the letter-box.... Still she didn't feel safe, so, in the end, without telling Ginger – it was the biggest and best surprise of his life – she made Mr Jones buy a dog. Biter (that was what Mrs Jones said the dog must be called) was huge, with the wolfish look of an Alsatian and the bay of a bloodhound. His nature was timid but affectionate. He loved Ginger, and Ginger loved him: Biter was Ginger's dog.

Write one sentence to say what *you* think about the story.

Draw a front cover for this story and write something for the back cover which will make children want to read it.

DROP EVERYTHING AND READ

ACKNOWLEDGEMENTS

The Authors and Publishers would like to thank the following for permission to reproduce copyright material:
The Bodley Head Ltd. for an illustration and extract from *The patchwork quilt* by Valerie Flourney, illustrated by Jerry Pickney, 1986, 'Early Bird does catch the fattest worm' from *Say it again Granny* by John Agard, 1986, and 'Three-hole' from *I din do nuttin* by John Agard; Cambridge University Press for illustrations and extract from *Legends of the animal world* by Rosalind Kerven, 1986; Collins Educational for extracts from *What's in a poem?* edited by Bill Boyle; J. M. Dent & Sons Ltd. for 'Cat and Mouse' from *The downhill crocodile whizz and other stories* by Margaret Mahy and front cover illustration by Ian Newsham; Andre Deutsch Ltd. for illustrations and extracts from *Jacob Two-Two and the dinosaur* by Mordecai Richler, 1975, *Jyoti's journey* by Helen Ganly, 1986, and 'Shut your mouth when you're eating' from *Quick, let's get out of here* by Michael Rosen, illustrated by Quentin Blake; Faber and Faber Ltd. for extracts 'Look out below' and 'The ghost hunter' from *Blue misty monsters* by Catherine Sefton, and illustration by Elaine McGregor-Turney, 1985; Roy Fuller for 'Autumn' from *Seen Grandpa lately*, Andre Deutsch, 1977 and 'In the bathroom' from *Poor Roy*, Andre Deutsch, 1977; Hamish Hamilton Ltd. for extracts and illustrations from *Panda's puzzle* by Michael Foreman, 1977, *The Hodgeheg* by Dick King Smith, 1987, and an extract from *Ramona Quimby, aged eight* by Beverly Clearly, 1981; Gregory Harrison for 'Are you pleased with the donkey you bought at the fair' from *A third poetry book*, Oxford University Press, and 'Distracted the mother said to her boy' from *A fourth poetry book*, Oxford University Press; William Heinemann Ltd. for the front cover and extracts from *Storm* by Kevin Crossley-Holland, 1985; Hodder & Stoughton Ltd. for cover of *Lend Me Your Wings* by John Agard, illustrated by Adrienne Kennaway; Macmillan Children's Books for extracts and illustrations from *The bedspread* by Sylvia Fair, 1986; Wes Magee for 'Giant rocket' from *A third poetry book*, Oxford University Press; Methuen Children's Books for the front and back covers of *Blue Misty Monsters* by Catherine Sefton, 1986; Spike Milligan Productions Ltd. for 'A baby sardine' and 'The terns' by Spike Milligan; William Morrow and Company, Inc. for illustrations from *There's nothing to do* by James Stevenson, Greenwillow Books, Copyright © 1986 by James Stevenson; New Directions Publishing Corporation for 'Hedgehog' by Chu Chen Po from *One hundred more poems from the Chinese* by Kenneth Rexroth, Copyright © 1970 by Kenneth Rexroth; Oxford University Press for the cover and 'Amanda' from *Snakes and ladders* by Robin Klein, 1985, and illustrations from *A second poetry book* and *A third poetry book* edited by John Foster, 1981; Penguin Books Ltd. for nine jokes from *The Puffin joke book* compiled by Bronnie Cunningham, Puffin Books. Copyright © 1974 by Bronnie Cunningham, 'Hedgehog', 'Rabbit' and 'Mouse' from *The big Peter Rabbit book*, Frederick Warne & Co. Copyright © 1986 by Frederick Warne & Co., covers illustrated by Caroline Binch from *The Elm Street lot* by Philippa Pearce, Puffin Books, 1987, covers illustrated by Peter Rush from *The Elm Street lot* by Philippa Pearce, Puffin Books, 1979, covers illustrated by Jon Riley from *Jacob Two-Two meets The Hooded Fang* by Mordecai Richler, Puffin Books, 1979, and one joke from *The ha ha bonk book* by Janet and Allan Ahlberg, Kestrel Books. Copyright © 1982 by Allan Ahlberg; A. D. Peters & Co. Ltd. on behalf of the author for 'Eye sore' from *Sky in the pie* by Roger McGough and Michael Rosen and Susanne Steel for 'Humm Tee Dim Tay'.

Every effort has been made to trace all the copyright holders but if any have been inadvertently overlooked the publishers will be pleased to make the necessary arrangement at the first opportunity.

© Sheila Freeman and Esther Munns 1989

All rights reserved. No reproduction, copy or transmission of this publication may be made without written permission.

No paragraph of this publication may be reproduced, copied or transmitted save with written permission or in accordance with the provisions of the Copyright Act 1956 (as amended), or under the terms of any licence permitting limited copying issued by the Copyright Licensing Agency, 33-4 Alfred Place, London WC1E 7DP.

Any person who does any unauthorised act in relation to this publication may be liable to criminal prosecution and civil claims for damages.

First published 1989

Published by MACMILLAN EDUCATION LTD
Houndmills, Basingstoke, Hampshire RG21 2XS
and London
Companies and representatives
throughout the world

Designed by Roger Walker/Linda Hardaker

Printed in Hong Kong

ISBN 0-333-45388-3

Illustrations: Norma Burgin pp 12, 13, 15; Terry Burton pp 11, 30, 31, 70, 71; Carolyn Bull pp 42, 43, 44, 45; Gareth Floyd pp 16, 17, 19, 66, 69, 74; Ian Heard pp 4, 5, 6, 7, 8, 9, 20, 24, 25, 29, 46, 47; Julie Hughes pp 75, 76, 77, 78, 79; Sebastian Quigley pp 36, 37, 38, 39, 40, 41; Cathie Shuttleworth pp 54, 55, 56, 57; Ursula Sieger pp 52, 53, 58, 60; Joyce Smith p 72. Cover illustration: Shirley Bellwood. Contents page: Russ Billington.